BE SELFISH

DURGESH STHALEKAR

© **Durgesh Sthalekar**

be Selfish

1st Edition
All rights reserved
Publication Date: October 2020
Price: ₹ 395 | $ 7.00
ISBN: 978-81-949155-6-0

Published by:
Adhyyan Books
Office No. 125,
Opposite Vivanta by Taj,
DDA SFS. Pocket-1, Dwarka,
Sec-22, New Delhi-110077
Website: http://adhyyanbooks.com
E-mail: contact@adhyyanbooks.com

I AM GRATEFUL TO YOU ALL FOR SUPPORT & CONTRIBUTION FOR THIS BOOK...

Rtn. Sunnil MEHRA, District Governor- Rotary Int. District 3141

Mr. Satyaki GHOSH, CEO - at Aditya Birla Group

Mr. Jagdish KINI, Business Coach

Mr. Sunu MATHEW, founder & MD LEAP INDIA Pvt.Ltd

Mr. Chintan VASANI, MD wisebiz

Mr. Pankaj MEHRA, Ex CEO Horizon Group- Estonia

Mr. Umesh MADHYAN, A.Vice president Logistics- Coca Cola

Ms. Ruchi UPADHYAY, DGM at VVF Group

Not to forget two women behind my progress & Happiness - Mother Sushila Sthalekar who is herself writer/Poet and

My wife Pooja , my moral support and my son Abhishek for inpiration to write on this subject...

How to use the Tips

We all have an ambition, Dream.

We want to grow and want more power.

We want to get that Promotion.

However, if we look at organization structure it becomes clear that we have many people at bottom and as you grow upwards, fewer positions!

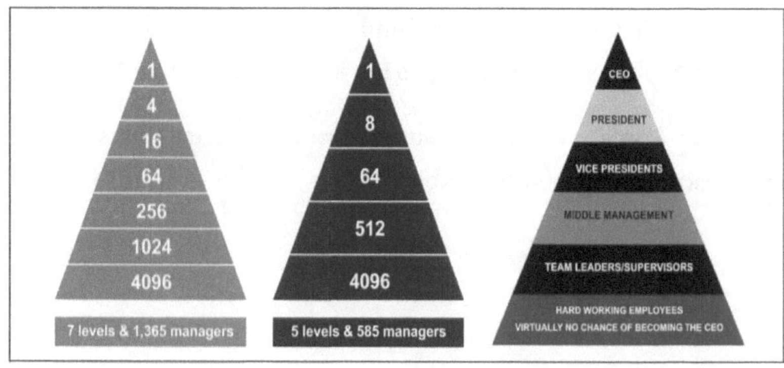

Tough competition?

Many sincere employees think that they will get a promotion if they work hard, perform their best.

Does that happen? Can a hard working salesman become a Sales Manager? Not really. Not just by working hard. So, how? Smart working?

Is an MBA degree enough for you to grow at work? Thousands of MBAs are churned out every year, do they all land up with Jobs as senior Managers? .....NO

Many fresh MBAs who joined us neither had any idea as to how the company's work (internally) nor any Institute cared to teach them. That's the problem with our education...hopefully new Education policy may bring in good change!

Well this book won't tell you how Sachin Tedulkar became 'God of Cricket' or what you can learn from Warren Buffett. Let's be clear...Celebrities don't run the country!

Why would you read this book?

Just as a practical guide. I'm happy with my success from salesman to General Manager. I am sharing my experience.

Well , success is different for every person. For some, success is marriage or having kids/starting business or closing it without losses. This book is about Promotion at work. One can plan his/her own career path...no one makes it for you. The book shares my experience and also tips from some top senior managers on 'career path'

If you are waiting for your company or boss will make your career path and you will walk on it to the top position.... You are completely wrong.

But IF you follow the tips I am giving, you have more brighter chances of getting promotion.

The book is divided in two parts ....

1. Personal Development mindset in challenging times- called **ID – Individual Development**
2. Developing emotionally to learn how to grow at work place called **SPG - strategic Plan for Growth**

For the benefit of yours, every tip is divided in a chapter. After reading each tip, think and note down how you will make use of your learning from it in real life. Think for 30 minutes on every chapter.

Think, Feel and Act cycle

The process of THINKING is constant within us, these thoughts drive us to make judgements about things around us and these judgements influence our feelings / emotions which translates into action. Without action (execution) there will be no success. Don't just build castles in the air, be ready to work hard!

It is said that you can change everything by just change in your thinking. I hope every tip here has the spark to start a new thinking process in your mind.

Make most of it

Remember this is about yourself so you must take maximum interest in your career first...

Durgesh Sthalekar

Individual Development-ID

Know yourself and you will win all battles

-Sun Tzu

CHAPTER 1

BE SELFISH, IT'S YOUR DREAM

In 2008, L'OREAL was going through the worst crisis. Falling Sales, financial indiscipline, stocks mismanagement, unhappy trade partners... The West Region was badly hit but others too had problems.

I was called by my division Director Vismay Sharma. He wanted to set things right and wanted me back in the sales team. I was working on a SAP project that time.

I knew very well what was happening in Market & the problem in the sales team. Vismay was correct on strategy but didn't get enough support in execution. Situation was very bad & completely mismanaged. But I was sure I could turn it around.

I agreed to take charge on one condition. I should be promoted as National Sales head and I will set everything right, starting from the West.

Was that right to keep my interest first than the company?

Well, it depends. I did that and my career took off.

I was promoted.

Vismay Sharma not only agreed but extended all support to me to restructure the sales team and we bounced back.

I worked hard to make sure we solved all problems in the next 6 months, including restructuring.

By doing that I helped myself, my boss and my company, too!

You have to be selfish ... to do good things.

Check whether you should be Selfish, too.

- How much time do you spend doing things for others but that are NOT important for you?
- Do you do a lot of work for others, but don't really get appreciated?
- You want to update your knowledge, learn more...but doesn't get time to do so? Busy fire fighting all the time
- You listen to others problems & help them but when you want to talk about yours, they have no time to listen?

If any of these situations sound familiar to you , you need to introspect and ...go to settings to make set "yourself as priority"

If that's called as being Selfish, so be it

You first

Before any flight, the announcement is made...

"If cabin pressure drops in the plane, the oxygen masks come out. Before helping anyone put the mask yourself first"

You know why?

Otherwise the person will begin to lose his or her ability to recognize faces and shapes, and eventually pass out. Hence, the flight-safety demo reminds passengers to take care of their own mask first.

That's not being selfish. It only states that "If you are not strong enough, you can't help others!" and that makes sense, isn't it?

You must value and respect your time. Set your own goals so that you can accomplish the important things. If you don't do this, then no one else will do it for you.

Your goals and dreams should come first in your life.

We all need to be selfish when it comes to work or career! You must have power first , then you help others. Why do people struggle so much for power? Yes, If you want to bring in any change ... power is essential.

However, to reach to that powerful position is tough journey and one has to be flexible, tolerant, calm and play positive politics

That's all we will go through in this book...

Everything Starts with YOU

China is building the world's first forest city filled with over one million Plants; well that's nothing new.

In India the Assam Forestry Division of Golaghat district planned to reforest 200 hectares of forest. As usual, the program was abandoned in 1983.

After that, **Jadav Payeng** single-handedly attended the forest. IN over 30 years he planted bamboo and other species to make 550 hectares of man-made forest.

Thanks to his efforts, the Molai forest now houses Bengal tigers, Indian rhinoceros, reptiles, over 100 deer and more.

He is called "Forest Man Of India"

Have you not heard of "Mountain Man of India" Dashrath Manjhi in Bihar? There is movie on his life MANJHI, you must watch

There are many stories around of brave men and women, who have fought odds and come out winners.

Let me give an example from my team.

Sunu Mathew, a hard working sales person joined L'Oreal in my team. He had that spark in his eyes and maybe an unidentified dream. He moved ahead in L'Oreal from frontline manager to be head of supply chain. While growing to higher positions, he also passed Post Graduation degree from IIM, Kolkata

What differentiated him from the rest was 'passion' and 'dedication' to perform better. I think he was competing with himself most of the time. His present was better than the past and future was perfectly planned.

Later he moved to CHEP India and finally started his own company LEAP INDIA Pvt. Ltd, which is worth Rs.1200 Crores now.

Sunu MATHEW is a success & inspiring story for all of us ... from a middle class family to be "founder & Managing Director" of a successful start-up !

Moral – Don't compete with friends and colleagues. Observe them, but compete with yourself. Make sure you are better year after year.

There are many such individuals who have succeeded in toughest conditions, look around 'your universe'.

You and your Universe

When we are born, our Universe starts there itself.

Your Family, relatives and social status. That's your Universe.

As you grow, you meet more people / friends and your universe grows. How much you want to grow in life depends on how much you expand your universe.

In this period, you consider some experts as Guru or you get influenced by someone... digitally or in your contacts. These are influencers. Your Father, your teacher , politician or businessmen or women around you.

Observe them, learn from them and think big.

What is your DREAM, does that have Purpose?

We dream almost every night and forget by morning.

Frankly, not everyone achieves their dream

Actor Boman Irani was room service attendant and Rajnikant was a bus conductor who did his job with extraordinary energy and got noticed.

For some, luck favours and for some, it doesn't. But everyone gets reward for trying... that's sure.

When you reach for the stars, you might not quite get one,
but you won't come up with a handful of mud either

- Leo Burnett

My brother, Vivek, started as a Real Estate Broker and over the time started advising everyone on making correct agreements. Over the period, he was known as an expert in making right agreements. Finally he did his LLB and now he is a successful lawyer.

So, focus on where you are and Where do you want to go.

If you don't reach the dream destination you will still be much better than what you were!

Isn't that better than not having any dream at all?

Purpose – the binding force

"Find Purpose: The means will follow"

-Mahatma Gandhi

Purpose differentiates between an average employee and a successful one. You should be very clear in your objective... what are you looking for in "success"

Money – Yes, everyone wants a fat salary. But that alone cannot be your dream.

Successful people have built big companies (Nandan Nilenkani & Narayan Murthy of Infosys) or made country proud (Virat Kohli, P.V.Sindhu) or have given big Box Office hits (Amir Khan, Akshay Kumar)

So, they have a bigger purpose to achieve and they worked hard on that. Money is bound to flow when you achieve your purpose.

I joined L'OREAL as Area Sales Manager when it was just 4.80 Crores and we worked very hard to make L'OREAL a top Beauty brand in India.

In 1997, no one knew L'OREAL in India. It was very difficult to find a distributor interested in our business.

Our team worked on personal rapport with trade. Whatever the tough time, we ensured that the brand image remains intact and with success of Hair Colors, we started our success journey.

Along with L'OREAL, I also grew in 22 years to be G.M of Luxury Division and the same is true with many colleagues of mine.

So, you should be playing active role in making your company great and at the same time keep your Dream alive

Moral - Make your Dream part of a bigger organisational purpose! While you drive the purpose, others join you. Indirectly others help you achieve your dream.

What others think about you? Let them

Please confirm if you experience any of the following...

1. Do you speak out? Or you keep your doubts with you for fear that you should not hurt someone

2. You're reluctant to say NO, so sometimes you say YES and do things you don't want to do

3. You think people avoid you

4. As you want to see everyone happy, you postpone taking decisions till everyone is OK

If your answer is YES to any one of the above, you are worrying too much about things. Frankly, there are many other important things you can do...other than worrying.

We have this bad habit of evaluating our success from others' feedback..what others think of you? How they look at you!

Here is How you change that thinking with new thinking...

<u>Who are these 'Others"?</u>

Everyone is busy with themselves.True . Most of the time, 'others' don't really think about you. They have their own challenges, dreams and they are fighting it out themselves.

But yes, there are few who have nothing to do but find faults in others. Leave them on their own. Don't try to change them. Waste of time!

Give time to yourself, rather.

When I was acting in a drama during college days. I used to get nervous after watching senior actors perform effortlessly. Chandrashekhar Vishwasrao, a respectable name in Marathi theatre was my guru.He came to me and said while you enter on stage, just think and tell yourself that "YOU are the best actor on stage ... unbeatable!" and act with confidence.It worked!

Actually, every senior actor was sincerely supportive. Problem was in my thinking.

My weak performance would have impacted their performance, too. So they wanted me to do better. When I changed my thinking, I was confident and performed better.

Remember, an actor's performance is remembered for a long time if the movie is a box office success. Every actor/ star knows this and they try to ensure that the rest of the team associated with the movie is best in class. Why not?

Moral – You are never alone. There is nothing called 'solo performance'. You have to admit and appreciate those who help you perform better. You also have a role to play in someone's struggle to achieve his or her dream.

Choose your Friends wisely

The 'Likes' on our Insta, facebook and Linkedin have taken significant importance in our life for no reasons.

All those who 'like' you in digital media will not be a real help in developing your career.

Try to choose friends who have some dreams, purpose in mind… those who love to think differently and spread positivity, like you! They could be a little senior to you, never mind.

Your friends circle can influence your thinking and hence future

Befriend the experts, successful people around you including your current or past bosses, entrepreneurs and join right platforms/clubs that help you build your contacts and expand the universe like Toastmasters, Rotary etc.

Rotary Club is one such place where you will get different minds from different fields. It offers you the best opportunity in learning leadership skills.

Make most of the "Present"

If you are not fully focused on current activity and not giving 100% to it, you are not on right track

Do you remember the Mutual Funds disclaimer?

Past performance of the schemes is neither an indicator nor a guarantee of future performance, and may not be considered as the basis for future investment decisions.

I just love this disclaimer, as it tells you how you should take life! Past experience is under past circumstances.

Don't let your 'past' influence your 'present'.

You are facing a different situation now, so observe things carefully and take action accordingly

Love yourself, be your own Fan

Do you want others to like you? Start with yourself.

It will build self-confidence. Take care of yourself. Go to the gym or walk for a minimum 30 minutes every day, spend some money to look better, Eat healthy food...

How to handle Critisism

" Critic be your neighbour"

–Saint (Sant) Tukaram

Some criticize 'you' and some 'your action'. Those who want you to do well criticize your action so that you change for better. Take it in right spirit, do introspection and improve.

Those who are jealous of you criticize you personally, leave them alone. They don't matter to you.

Similarly, please do not criticize a person individually, you may criticize an action or a decision.

You can't make everyone Happy!

We had an Area Manager Deepak Laver based at Pune...man with a golden heart. He loved everyone, his team and his trade partners. He would walk an extra mile for everyone. He would accompany his team members to market and help them sell more to achieve their targets.

But that happened often. Everyone knew Deepak would be there to help him or her so why work hard? Retailers knew that Deepak would meet them at month-end and offer extra discounts then why buy from his team members?

While making everyone happy, Deepak got overstrained. It became a one-man show and unmanageable. We had to move him to Nagpur.

Moral - You must know that you can't please everyone; it's just not possible. People have expectations; they judge you with those expectations in mind. If you try to make everyone happy, you will never be able to do anything big.

Listen to everyone, but listen more carefully to yourself.

Follow your gut ....

WOW, Words Of Wisdom

Sunu MATHEW
MD & Founder – LEAP
INDIA PVT LTD

I would like to dedicate my life to the word "Courage".

From leading my school's sports team to

travel alone in Delhi for studies to

marrying my Girl friend ahead of my elder brother to

come and start a business in Mumbai to

agreeing for streamlining the operations of L'Oreal – Srilanka to

joining Supply Chain when I was doing well in Business Management to

leave L'Oreal when I was at the peak and

join CHEP and then

finally leaving the company to start LEAP.

Do not carry the past with you.

Leader should have the ability to "Forget & Forgive" – this will allow you to generate better ideas as your subconscious mind is clear and does not carry any baggage of the past

From the above message of Mr. Sunu Mathew, you will notice an interesting thing. He decided to move ahead, change gears of his career path when he was at the top of it and not at bottom.

Just like surfers in the sea who enjoy riding on the wave...that's courage!

If you take responsibility for yourself, you will develop a hunger to accomplish your dreams

–Les Brown

CHAPTER 2
TAKE RESPONSIBILITY

What is 'being responsible'?

No jargon.

How a salaried driver drives his owner's car? Now suppose he starts his own OLA car, how will he drive and maintain his own car?

Difference in staying / decorating a rented home & your own home? What is the difference?....

OWNERSHIP

It's natural behaviour. When you feel you are responsible for something, you take the ownership and when you own something, you take care!

Take care of your career and Life, too!

It's your Life! When you make any decision about yourself, you are responsible for it.

I am NOT a product of my Circumstances. I am a product of my decisions

–Unknown

So, what do you do EXACTLY to take responsibility or ownership?

Don't blame others for your decisions

You are responsible for every decision you take. You may consult family, friends or experts but whatever you finally chose is your decision.

If the decision works out good, you gain. But if a decision fails you, you should not blame others. As stated earlier, everything starts with you!

In my team, there was this executive Sunil, very aggressive & ambitious. He could accept any challenging targets & push himself to achieve it. But he was poor in strategy and maturity so couldn't get that promotion.

Every successful sales person cannot be a Manager

But he was ambitious so he left Job to start his distribution business. We offered him our Brand as we had confidence in him. Initially, it was good business but as he saw high cash flow, which he had never seen before, he started to invest in stocks (Equity) & started a travel operator business too. Too many priorities created problems for him.

He lost brands, travel business and booked losses in stocks too.

Later, got into banking fraud case and ended his career (almost)

Problem is not failure but playing the victim card and blaming circumstances or others for the fall. There was no change in his attitude despite all this and the bad days continued.

Moral - Take responsibility for your failures, introspect and admit your mistakes. Make necessary corrections and start on the right path again.

Never play victim card (I am victim of _ _ , I was misdirected by _)

Those feelings may be correct. You might have been conned and hence you may feel bad, but such feelings won't help you.

The truth is this: Your life is not about them. It's about you.

You need to stop blaming <u>so that</u> you can fight back and win

Hate excuses

Roy was always late for meetings and also visiting markets. However, every time he had some 'reasons' for being late! He could justify that with fervor. But no one would buy his argument.

His team members lost respect for him and he lost opportunities for his future. What he gave were his reasons but for everyone it was excuses!

Moral- justifying mistake is an excuse. Success doesn't need justification.

We all make mistakes. In fact, when you are trying something new... you may commit mistakes. If you are not making any mistakes in Life, you better watch your career. Maybe you are doing mundane work, doing as directed.

Every mistake teaches you something

When you make excuses, you opt not to learn from your mistakes.

Excuse brings in negativity with it, maybe because you have to blame someone or situation.

When you take responsibility for your life and stop making excuses, you silence the negativity.

Go for GOOD HABITS... Discipline yourself

Your habits indicate your mindset. Do you agree?

How habits are formed? You follow a particular way of life diligently because that makes you feel better. Some things energize you, make you happy and hence you love to do it again and again.

Habits are habits, if they are not destroying your health or career, then it's good habit. If you are disciplined, you are closer to your goals.

Mr. Pankaj MEHRA was the commercial director and my boss when I was RSM in L'OREAL. He was well respected in trade as well as by his team for his knowledge, empathy and commitment.

Moreover he is a disciplined person. He would spend good time with his team in the evening but next day work starts sharp at 9 am. Work hard, party hard!

He would keep his word and practice what he preached. We learned discipline and integrity from him.

People who follow discipline have complete control over themselves.

Best way to take responsibility for your life is with your daily habits.Are your daily habits helping you improve your life?

Are you taking care of your body, your mind, and your needs?

Here are all the ways that you could be taking responsibility for your mind and body:

◦ Sleep properly and wake up early, for fresh day

◦ Eat healthy, enjoy life but be in limits

◦ Giving yourself 30 min everyday to think about your life

◦ Exercise regularly, 30 min a day?

◦ Gratitude - Thank yourself and those around you

◦ Playing sport when you can, develop sporting spirit

◦ Reading a book

We all are little Negative and Lazy

This one is tricky

There is no one without Negative thoughts. Some sort of negative thinking is there in everyone sometimes.

We must accept this fact and take responsibility for our negative emotions by controlling them rightly. The negative emotions/ experiences that we have stored in our mind affect us.

Procrastination – The result of our negative experiences can lead to a habit of Procrastination (Merriam Webster Dictionary meaning --to put off intentionally the doing of something that should be done)

We make plans but always avoid them. Thus, we postpone to START. Many decide to leave their job and start to do something on their own ...but that 'something' remains secret for long.

Why? Maybe some worries, some past negative experience, Laziness, fear of failure and the fact that 'something' is not clear to them also!

Action Speaks...the most important and critical part of taking responsibility is action. In corporate language it is called 'execution'

You are the first person responsible for achieving your dream and hence you need to face your owns doubts, sort them out and start taking action

Moral – Don't let negative thoughts take charge of you. Do not delay taking decisions and acting on it for fear of failure. Follow your instinct. Failure is not the end, it is the beginning of change

Chintan Vasani
Founder and Managing Partner at Wisebiz Realty

<u>3-key areas to focus on</u> for career or business growth

1. Collaborate

The most important thing today to thrive your business and grow professionally for any individual is to identify your best abilities and team up or collaborate with like minded individuals and other talents. You can only reach till a point if you go alone, you need to join hands and grow together to reach greater heights.

2. Patience and Planning

In my past experience, I have realised the importance of planning for months for an execution of a few weeks. Invest your time and resources in research and planing. This will surely bear fruits and post a full proof plan and a good execution, you do need patience. Things work out or else they fall apart to male way for better things.

3. Look at the larger picture and Self Belief!

Whatever work you are doing, plan to 2X or 4X the same in phased manner. This will help you to work harder and will always keep you motivated. Self Belief is the most important super power one can have. Always respect the financial investments of your company or your investor as your own fund and always do justice to it!

Abundance is not something we acquire. It is something we tune into

–Wayne Dyre

CHAPTER 3

ABUNDANCE MINDSET, GET YOUR SLICE!

Abundance mindset

There are these two types of mindsets- abundance and scarcity

As they sound, scarcity mentality makes the person self-doubting.

Focused on envying on what others have and what they don't. They will never look happy. In every situation they will see problems or impediments. Scarcity brings in insecurity, sometimes for no reason.

Against this, Abundance Mentality brings in thinking that there is enough for everyone. They look at what they have and make it stronger. They want to play on their strengths rather than wasting time on correcting their weaknesses. Abundance teaches you to respect everyone, as they believe there is something to learn from everyone.

Rajubhai Kotecha, the owner of Mumbai's oldest Distribution house Jethalal Meghji & Co. is ever smiling and a happy man. They have been in business for more than 4 decades. He is an abundance man. He has worked with many good Brands. He has seen bad times with some of his people duping him for millions but he doesn't discuss it.

He thinks whatever is gone did not belong to him.

Abundance mindset has given him freedom to interact with his customers with an open mind without worrying about profits. Profit remains byproduct and he is still doing very well.

People want to do business with him. That's most important.

You would always like to do business with an energetic person who brings in positivity rather than a complainer who starts with 'problems & complaints' whenever he/ she opens mouth

When you have abundance mindset, you see opportunities, you are open to collaboration and your creativity flows

How do you get an abundance mentality?

Simple, first know what is scarcity mentality symptom...

1. When someone is successful and gives you happy news, you feel that ..."it's not he/she but I deserved it"

2. You have this feeling "I am not lucky enough"

3. When someone fails, you feel comfortable inside...

4. You always compare what you have got with others, maybe salary increments, gifts from someone... and feel that you have been ignored

5. You want to give in charity, when you have enough...but you never have enough

6. You want to win every game...

7. You are focused on today & now; don't like to discuss long-term goals/ dreams as if there is no tomorrow.

How do you go Abundance?

Observe good things around us

Look at our lives and how we are getting better..

✔ Life expectancy is rising ...

✔ GDP is growing every year... (Except this year due to Coronavirus, maybe)

✔ Poverty is reducing, falling rate of suffering due to hunger, more children are going to school

✔ Chances of war are minimal as most countries are nuclear powers

✔ Technology making life's better, comfortable

✔ Average income of people growing

✔ More opportunities, more start-ups, more financers

So, there is enough for everyone! Be sure.

I travelled from North to south and some wonderful towns of Northeast. Not for holidays, but for business.

It was amazing to find loyal consumers for beauty products in every small town I visited. We had customers for L'OREAL everywhere! They are willing to pay a premium price for quality.

Also, there are so many local brands in every state who have been delivering quality products to local customers and these brands are looking forward to go National

So, please don't watch 'breaking news' Channels and feel pessimistic. Look around you and you will find inspiring stories… be one of them.

We all have a habit of finding faults, that's how we were tuned.

"If you look at what you have in life, you will always have more. If you look at what you don't have in life, you will never have enough."

-Oprah Winfrey

ACTION -Start finding good things in people that you know. Write down in your book. Similarly note down good things about your company, society etc.

Do what you love to do

Some of the things we love to do and some we have to do.

If you are not happy with what you are doing, you will be watching the clock every time to get away.

Having said that, not everyone is lucky to get the job they want. Thus, there will be struggle. You should give justice to every work you are doing, while doing so you will start liking the new job too!

After spending 5 years as Regional Manager in the West, I was asked to take charge of North. I was told that this exposure could help me for the next level. I didn't agree with the view but accepted relocation.

When I traveled across the North, I found my team was very open-minded. The year was great success and as a team we bonded well. The relocation helped me actually.

Next year I moved again back to Mumbai for the S.A.P project as Key Advisor. From a managing team of 150 people, I was here with no team. Now everything has changed. From operations to SAP was tough. I had to get my project done through interacting with the team, which was not reporting to me.

Moreover, I had to suggest a lot of new ways of working to them, as Key user of SAP. Change always brings inconvenience and no one likes it. However, I enjoyed this too. From boss to team member... This job taught me to be humble and take people with you for a purpose, not power!

In every work you do, there will be learning. If you move to a new department or relocate to a new town, take it as a project for new learning. Don't get distracted from your dream though!

ACTION – note down all activities that you carry out in your current position. Find out which activity is close to your strengths or something you would love to do. Go for it. Focus on one activity every month.

Giving for loving

I moved to Myanmar, met my team there and my beautiful journey started.

In the Human Development Index, Myanmar ranked 150 in 187 countries. It is an under-developed country economically. But it has got fertile soil and abundant water sources so the agricultural conditions are best. It's a food surplus country and you know ... Myanmar is ranked No. 1 in 'world giving Index'. How? There are three parameters on which a survey is done for "giving index ranking" ...

1. Helped a stranger, or someone they didn't know who needed help?

2. Donated money to a charity?

3. Volunteered your time to an organization?

Truly, If you travel across Myanmar you will experience empathy, respect and loving people. Money can't buy everything.

If you are positive in these three areas, you are going the Abundance way!

ACTION – Decide that every month you will help for some cause, as per your capacity...do something that brings a smile on someone's face. You will feel great seeing that smile.

Be Open Minded

If you go by that closed mindset, you block all possibilities of learning.

"I know all" is common, get out of it.

ACTION: Decide to learn something new ... It can be a hobby like painting or language. Join any course from online academies or see classic movies in other languages (with subtitles!)

Express Gratitude

There are certain things in our mind by which we take things as granted. We don't express our gratitude for what we are getting.

Whether it's family, friend, colleague or boss... express gratitude for every good thing you are getting from them. Don't forget GOD!

"When you are grateful, fear disappears and abundance appears."

– Tony Robbins

ACTION – start the practice of expressing gratitude by heart to people around you.. Just say # Thank you very much! # So nice of you! # Appreciate your help...from your family members to boss, office assistant, delivery boy or security guards

Satyaki GHOSH
**CEO - Domestic Textiles & Thai Acrylic Fibre at ADITYA BIRLA Group
Director, Consumer Products Division
L'OREAL INDIA**

My mantra for 'career development' is essentially:

1) Keep focussed – decide what you want to be, plan how to get there and then follow that plan. Career is like a 'Treasure hunt'...

a) First, there has to a treasure!! That's what you need to decide.. what is your treasure... otherwise you will keep hunting and never get it.. because you don't know what is your treasure!! (not everyone wants to be CEO.. what does success look like for you is the key here)

b) Second, you must have a map to find the treasure. Be prepared, plan well. That's your map. If there is no map then you will not reach the treasure even if there is one!

c) Lastly, ask yourself everyday if you are working towards your plan. Remain focussed on the end game and continuously upgrade yourself to reach your goal (treasure)

2) Be flexible – Rigidity never helps... if something is logical and doesn't take you away too much from your master plan then please accommodate changes... remember 'change is the only constant' in this VUCA world.

3) Network well – The corporate world is becoming flatter... hierarchies are reducing and a more matrix organisation is

emerging. This means much higher levels of collaboration, cross functional teamwork. 'Influencing' will be the key as opposed to 'directing' and this is where 'networking' kicks in. More you know how to get your work done through your network (within and outside the organisation) and by 'influencing'.. more successful will you be.

If u want to work in corporate,

then u should know how to play chess.

—Honeya

CHAPTER 4
PLAY POSITIVE POLITICS, CAREFULLY

What is office politics?

Politics is present virtually in all places in the world. Our offices are not different either. In most cases, people engage in office politics to mostly further their agenda and to gain the benefit at any cost. Nevertheless, there are some good aspects to it too.

Engaging in Office Politics:

Though most of the people consider office politics to be a despicable thing, you may find it wise to engage in it carefully.

The most important thing you must know...never play bad politics with your boss, even if he is playing it.

Actively engaging in good office politics is a way to get you noticed and make a positive impact. But how will you do it?

1. How to distinguish between good and bad office politics:

Before you get actively involved in office politics, I think it is better to understand the distinction between good and bad office politics.

Well, bad office politics mostly involve manipulation, backstabbing, spreading rumours and similar morally wrong deeds. Thus, engaging in these activities can harm you as well as others around you. On the other hand, good politics involves advancing your interests while ensuring the best for the organisation too.

When I joined L'OREAL, it was a very exciting atmosphere. L'OREAL was fighting tough market conditions. Ultra DOUX (shampoo) had failed.

Our sales director resigned and Regional Manager of North Mr. Pankaj MEHRA was promoted as Sales Director. Some colleagues could not digest the development. I was Area Manager! My boss thought that I was a pro-Sales Director. Actually, I was pro-business. I overcame my boss's hostile behavior by aligning with Mr. Pankaj MEHRA. I played the positive politics of getting help from him for my team. All our initiatives helped us grow higher and helped team-West also.... Helping my boss (RSM-West) indirectly.

2. Engage in good politics only:

It is never wise to jump on the office politics bandwagon without having a solid plan. You may unknowingly get engaged in negative politics and it will be hard to break-free of that.

One must have four basic skills for practising good politics. That's ...

✔ social astuteness,

✔ networking ability,

✔ interpersonal influence and

✔ apparent sincerity.

They indicate you must be self-aware and know how others see you while maintaining a cordial and honest relationship thereby influencing the decision-making process of others.

3. Be political only for a higher purpose:

As someone who has first-hand experience in experiencing office politics, let me tell you that you must engage in it only to serve a higher purpose. It may never come as selfish...rather you must frame it as completely selfless and in the best interest of the organisation.

That is something I think you need to establish in order to foster good politics and navigate through the office hierarchy easily.

Unfortunately, I met a similar boss in the Luxury division who was all into himself. Interestingly, even he could not last long at any position

Moral – When you play politics in corporate life for personal gain without any skill, intelligence and ethical support, you actually work to end your career in that organization. Never deviate your objective, it has to be growth of organization and with it... your growth.

Please observe your boss carefully and work out a strategy to manage him accordingly. We will talk more on this in MAPPING

. . .

Tricks to conquer bad office politics:

• One thing that every individual must do to protect them from ugly politics is to maintain friendly and cordial relationships with colleagues. There is always strength in unity. So, by standing together with your colleagues, you will be able to discourage any individual trying to engage in negative politicking and expose their misdeeds.

We had wonderful HR directors in L'OREAL all along and everyone knew on-going politics in every division. They always made sure that the right person does not suffer even though they could not stop bad promotions, sometimes!

• **Keep a tab on the work you do**. There will always be few people that try to hog all the credit for the work you do in front of others. Try not to let that continue. Record or file everything that you are doing for your organisation officially. Most importantly, report to your superiors from time to time for everything you did. It will help you to maintain your reputation and image in the organisation. Communicate effectively...

• **Never say anything bad about someone who is not present...** This is more badmouthing. No one is a close friend in corporate life. Read about Rotary's 4 way test at the end of this step..

• Lastly, **take wise steps, never retaliate abruptly**. While working in a corporate culture, I had a vilifying experience of working with a certain person who always tried to belittle me in every step. It was horrifying for me and it surely filled me with anger.

Don't forget that you cannot act out of anger. Rather, it is important to keep calm and take wise steps. You may confront them individually and try reason with them. Even if it does not work, they will be careful before making a wrong move.

I always asked my boss for a drink together where I would explain my views/ position and clear misunderstanding.

Note, here drink is not important but discussion is. Therefore do not get emotional. You may have a coffee, too. That's actually better!

Rtn Sunnil Mehra
District Governor 2020-21
Rotary International
District 3141

In the early 1930s, Herbert Taylor was going through a bad phase in his business, he decided to change the ethical standards of his organisation.

The first job he set out to do is design a set of policies, to reflect high ethical values. It seems, as the story goes, he could not get it right by himself. He then leaned upon his faith in the almighty and coined the next few words.

Of all the things we think, say or do

"THE FOUR WAY TEST"

1. Is it the truth?

2. Is it fair to all concerned?

3. Will it build goodwill and better friendships?

4. Will it be beneficial to all concerned?

After applying it to himself, he later shared it with his organisation's heads of department. They endorsed the same in spite of having different cultural beliefs, and spread it to the entire organisation. Within years of this four way test, Herbert Taylor had paid his debts, and was back on a healthy track

It was here that he designed what was later to be known as the Four Way Test.

In 1940 when he became Rotary International Director, he offered it to Rotary and in order to align with the ethos of Rotary, the Four Way Test was adopted. The test can be applied to nearly every aspect of life

Rotary is an organisation which was formed in 1905, by a group of four Americans, led by Paul Harris.

Today Rotary International is the world's largest NGO, known for its ethics and integrity. It has been rated with a four star rating (the highest) by Charity Navigator for the last so many years.

Skill in the art of communication is crucial to a leader's success. He can accomplish nothing unless he can communicate effectively.

–Norman Allen

CHAPTER 5

COMMUNICATE EFFECTIVELY

We communicate by means of voice-language, gestures and signs. Professor of psychology Albert Mehrabian studied the importance of non-verbal communication, which is very strong.

He developed a model of communication which states that only 7% of what we communicate consists of the message. The use of tone, voice and volume take up 38% and as much as 55% of communication is body language. That's 7 – 38 – 55 –Mehrabian model of communication.

So its not what we say but how we say is important and while doing so how is our posture matters most.

We communicate through body language. That makes it important as how you present yourself.

You need not be in a formal suit all the time but a clean, fresh and energetic look with a broad smile can make a difference. Your mannerism, etiquettes convey a lot about you. How you behave with others, especially juniors, tells about your culture and you command respect accordingly.

Whether its professional or personal life, communication skills can make your image.

Here are some tips for you...

Listen carefully -

Well you will be surprised that the most important thing in communication is to listen.

Listen carefully to understand what someone is saying, ask questions if you find a few words hard to understand. You may rephrase and say " So you mean to say_______ right?" That makes the other person more happy that you are listening seriously.

Do not interrupt and start giving solutions to people. Most of the time, they are not seeking your advice... just speaking out.

They already know the solution, perhaps!

Avoid gossiping. If discussions move to criticizing the boss or someone... change the topic.

If someone is talking about you or your team, don't become a defensive listener. Defensive listeners listen to note points and defend their position later.

Listen to understand the other viewpoint clearly. You may get some good idea.

There is a wrong notion that a salesperson has to talk a lot. The new mantra is that you should listen to your customer and find out what he/she wants and then (talk) start your selling to meet that requirement

. . .

Think well before you speak out

Don't shoot the messenger. Have you heard this?

A messenger came to an Armenian king to tell him of a Roman conqueror advancing towards them, the king punished the messenger by cutting his head. Post that no one gave any intelligence message to King and he had to face war without being prepared.

Hence it later became unwritten code that during any war ' a messenger / emissary cannot be killed by opposing sides'

In corporate life,many bosses welcome flattering feedback but can't digest negative feedback/ news.

I had this chat with one of my MD, I was clearly giving him feedback on the market scenario and where we failed. L'Oreal showed negative growth for the first time in 2008 and he was new to India. He sincerely appreciated my feedback. Why, because I was referring to his predecessor's time!

After 2 years, he didn't like any critical feedback on company strategies or marketing plans!

Because I was giving feedback on his plans!

So, be careful when you speak. Read the situation first.

Don't give bad news straightaway, talk about few positive developments and then call failures as … improvement areas

Pay attention to your body language

Don't get too obsessed about it, but do make sure that you don't show your nervousness through body language.

Be relaxed. Open arms, relaxed legs and posture with a friendly tone will make you approachable and will help you build your network.

Use light and Fresh aquatic perfume like OGA Aqua Blue (Men) or OGA Hypnotique (women) EDP during office time. Make it a habit to smell good!

Keep eye contact but don't stare. Practice Empathy

Shake hands firmly but not to show your strength.

E-mails

Currently Emails are replacing every kind of communication in corporate life. People sitting next to each other also communicate through Email.

The purpose of Email was to communicate with people at your time, when you are free. If things are urgent, we pick up our mobile and call or walk to each other's desk and talk.

But, nowadays many are taking Email as the most urgent. They spend most of the time on mail. You will never have quality time to work on important issues if you want to respond to every mail immediately.

Prioritize.

ACTION - Attend Training program on Public Speaking which will boost your confidence and ability to present in front of people. Learn Presentation skills

Pankaj MEHRA

Former CEO- Horizon Tissues, ESTONIA
General Manager – L'OREAL
Professionnel Products Div
General Manager- CPD, ViETNAM

I have always believed that the two most important traits or attitudes required to succeed in life are discipline and perseverance.

As a leader of a young sales team in the initial years at L'Oreal I always felt that one of the most important tasks was to create an environment which would facilitate each member to perform to the fullest or contribute even beyond one's abilities. The two most important ingredients required for creating that environment are discipline and perseverance.

Discipline to me allows one to remain and keep focus on team results and objectives. It eliminates ambiguity, helps overcome fear, promotes the notion of fairness by bringing in transparency and fosters productivity and efficiency. The various dimensions of Discipline are to do with managing time, being organized, following process, delivering on benchmarks, propriety & ethical behavior and appearances. As a leader one's responsibility is to build with the team some rules, define clear goals and outline acceptable behavior. The implementation requires definition, participation, clarification and most critically leading by example at each level of hierarchy within the organization. We got about building discipline at L'Oreal by creating a consensus around acceptable behavior right from defining grooming, starting meetings on-time and establishing ethical practices on distributor (customer) engagement.

Perseverance to me is all about passion, stamina and sticking with your goals. It is about "consistent effort and conscious practice". The ability to persevere propels you towards action and gives you energy to get you up every time you are down or you have setback. The ability to carry on requires one to be optimistic, have hope and as a result have a positive outlook. This again is a trait which one develops when you constantly challenge yourself. As leader it is one's responsibility that you build an environment, along with the team members, of encouragement and positive outlook. As you persevere you would make mistakes, you are entitled to and you must make mistakes.... ensure you learn from your mistakes and never to repeat the same mistake again.

However both Discipline and Perseverance does not imply suppressing talent, disparage creativity or taking out element of fun while pursuing objectives and goals. On the contrary a disciplined organization which perseveres achieves goals in the most productive and efficient manner ......leaving team members with less fatigue and more time to have fun and hone both their talent and creativity. In addition it nurtures and promotes team spirit and camaraderie.

As a leader it is important to recruit, integrate, endorse and retain individuals who show traits of being disciplined and persevering.

*"Those who follow the crowd usually get lost in it.
I don't know all the keys to success, but one key to
failure is to try to please everyone."*

—Rick Warren

CHAPTER 6
DON'T FOLLOW THE CROWD EVERY TIME

Follow the crowd

Most of us want to go by the crowded street where we are sure we will not get lost, particularly if you are in a new town. Likewise youngsters follow a career path that's currently in demand... it was engineering, medicine then IT professionals, Marketing now.

Students want to go to IIM, IIT to get a degree and a lucrative campus offer of 1 crore a year.

This is changing now with people wanting to go for start-up ... Not seeking jobs but creating jobs. This is the road less traveled

So, the new mantra is "Never follow the crowd" or "Taking the road less traveled". That means in Hindi... "Hat ke" thinking!

Here you are acting independently, not following standard guidelines laid down years ago.

Well this book is not for entrepreneurs but for those who want to grow at work. Hence, I recommend that you understand the corporate meaning of ' being different' or 'Innovation'

Companies follow standard Operating Procedures (SOPs) for many internal workings and systems are designed on it. There are internal HR rules & ethics that help everyone work systematically. Just like law & Order of a state, you should follow the crowd for these guidelines.

There are area's where the goal is important and the process cannot be defined. Ask yourself "Can there be better way to do the thing which will be more effective, cost efficient, reliable and maybe quicker to execute?"

We at L'Oreal had the tough task of defining channels to sell Beauty Products, being first in category. I always believed that India is a huge market but reaching every small town is difficult and hence we need wholesale. I was the first to activate key wholesalers for L'Oreal make-up and later I encouraged my team (West Region) to expand distribution and activate wholesale for GARNIER. I was an exception and hence faced difficulties for doing so. But I knew that we need wholesalers.

When Satyaki Ghosh joined L'Oreal as my boss, he changed the path of L'Oreal from just Beauty to FMCG. That changed everything to put us on a fast track of growth.

I am proud that I had started driving that change first...now that road is crowded.

Moral – Be bold in what you stand for. If you are sure about your ideas and have honest intentions, you will get appreciated sooner or later.

Two things you should be ready for when you propose to try a new way...

CHANGE

Change is not easy. Every time you suggest change, you must have studied the subject fully and be confident to be successful for the new way! Your plan would be questioned and doubts will be raised. But that's right. While making a plan, you must anticipate questions. Check what are the probable answers and be ready with explanations

MISTAKES

When you are working on finding better ways and trying them, you will commit mistakes. How you handle them is important.

I have gone through many situations of embarrassment due to initiatives taken by me.

> *The rate at which a person can mature is directly proportional to the embarrassment he can tolerate.*
>
> **-Douglas Engelbart**

You should be willing to admit that you have made mistakes...

Own the mistake – you will not be able to learn anything from your mistake if you don't own it.

You can show maturity by not blaming someone else for your mistake. While it takes courage to say sorry for the mistake, please say so and assure that you have learnt from it. That will make others more confident about you.

If you are sure that the goal that you wanted to achieve is valuable... try again differently and never give up.

First find your strengths

You need to know yourself better before you decide how you want to make impact in the organization.

Play on your strengths, don't waste time on correcting weaknesses. Be confident in what you have decided to go for...

Now take SPG Cover!
STRATEGIC PLAN FOR GROWTH

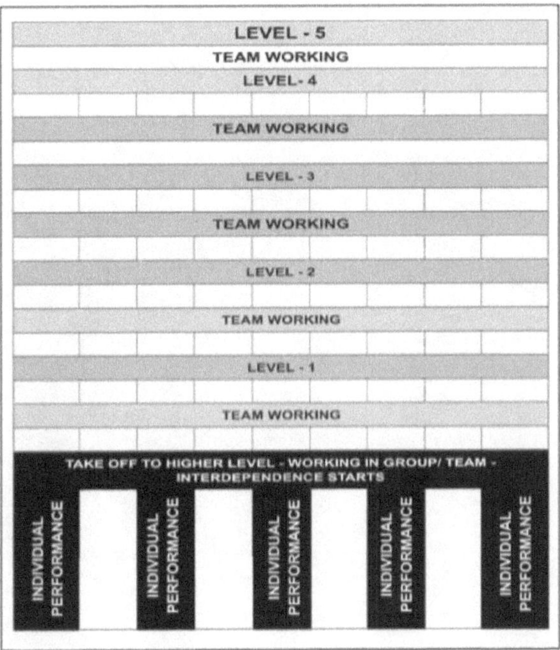

As you can see the diagram, you are 'Individual performer' when you join the organisation. You are responsible for your individual performance only. You can spend 3 to 4 years proving yourself.

But to cross the first level and take-off to managerial level, you must learn how to work with people to achieve your goal.

A level up, you will be dealing with other departments, their teams and get their cooperation to help your team achieve the goal...the higher you go, bigger is your team!

Master the art of observing

CHAPTER 7

MAPPING

Know your terrain first – company culture

What is Mapping: in a war situation, one must know the terrain. Before battle begins, opposing sides collect all information on the enemy. The prior military intelligence on enemy firepower, deployment of forces, supply chain support etc helps in making battle plans.

The classic book " The art of war by Sun Tzu explains it.

For us terrain is ' structure and culture' of the company you are working for. You must know the corporate world around you in which everyone competes to grow. What is company culture?

The values, practices and beliefs that govern the company's

decision making & working processes becomes culture

Culture of the company is very important. The culture is developed over the period of time by the way the management behaves with reporting teams and same going down till frontline team members

One can do nothing but accept the office culture as a reality. It is imperative to acknowledge and understand office culture before making any plans for self growth. You need at least one year to know company culture.

Decision makers

Understand your office hierarchy and identify who the real influencers are. Your boss will always play major role in your growth, whether he is smart or stupid. You can't choose your boss, so find out how your boss is. Ambitious? Well connected at top? Seniors like him/her or not?

If your boss is ambitious, you have an opportunity to grow but if you observe that he/she is not going ahead in Life & Stuck at that level for long? You have a problem

Check your team. What are the strengths of each team member? Is anyone in your team blue-eyed boy/girl of your boss? How can you be the one? Match your strengths with the liking of your boss.

You must have someone in HR as your friend. Not that the person will help you to get promoted but, you can get some inputs on what's going on in the company.

Promotion process -

How does promotions happen in your company? Study the last few promotions done to find out why someone was promoted?

Is there any assessment test, group discussions etc carried out for promotions? If yes, you need to be prepared. Ask a few who have attended this process, it can enlighten you. Also then you know who takes final interviews.

MBA degree – Unfortunately, many companies have made this a filter... having an MBA degree. It is better that you work hard and get that degree. Whichever University, but not having one can be a bigger obstacle.

Gifting – This is interesting and it helps. You need not give expensive gifts. In fact, you should never do that as the link with your ambition and gift will become clear. People will avoid you. Rather find interesting souvenirs / mementos to give to some select people whenever you go to interesting places for holiday or work. Seniors will appreciate that... but keep in mind, not very expensive.

Don't work on clock

Reach the office before 15 minutes and leave after office closure timing. Be disciplined. Be exactly on-time for every meeting. If you are late someday, do apologize for being late.

✔ Criteria for promotion

There are three areas that you should work on to get the promotion. I will give their weightage, too. But it may change as per the company....

1. Performance – 30% weight. Why so low? Frankly, if you are to be short-listed for promotion, performance will be basic criteria. Everyone will be almost at par. But don't be under the impression that the best performer has more chances..... No. This is not your written test exams!

2. Personal Branding – 30% Weight. Yes. You are also a brand. How is your packaging (dressing, personality) , communication , marketing, promotion, public relations.... All that matters!

3. Networking & exposure- 40% weight. Maybe you will feel this %age is unbelievable. But that's a fact. If you have done your branding well and meet the right people regularly, they can give positive feedback about you which will help.

We will talk about these criterias separately. .. except performance which is basic and depends on your efforts.

When I was in North, Mr.Rajesh VOHRA was my ASM. His knowledge on Market, competition, trade partners, consumer behaviour was extraordinary. He had strong positivity in him which would inspire the whole team and his colleagues, too.

He was open minded to learning . He could interact with marketing with ideas and implement the same in his area effectively. He was not just a good manager but a good trainer, motivator and developed good rapport with everyone.

More interestingly, he succeeded in every task assigned to him. Obviously, he had to grow. Today he is C.E.O of ARTSANA India.

Even individuals need to develop a brand for themselves …whatever your area of expertise, you can take steps to make people think of you when they think of your field

–Accelepoint Webzine

CHAPTER 8
DEVELOP BRAND 'YOU'

While I was managing All India sales Shaamain joined our selective Beauty channel as sales manager. She was very aggressive so there were frictions in the team. I had to meet her and explain the company culture. Sometimes when people join from other companies, they take some time to adjust to the new culture. She moved to Marketing where she was aggressive too.

Later She was given E-commerce and wow! At that time E-Commerce was very small and she took up the challenge at the right time!

Her aggressive strategies worked well with the market which was also growing very fast. E-com became the highest growing and profitable channel in L'Oreal for her efforts.

Today, she is promoted and enjoys greater challenges out of India.

What helped her? She was known as "aggressive taskmaster"...
this kind of Branding helped her when people were looking for
someone like that to manage E-com channel

So, what's a "brand"?

A brand is a recognizable name that distinguishes you in a
crowded market. Imagine if someone calls your (say Andy)
friends and ask them "how can you describe Andy? How is he?"

Now whatever they say ..."Andy is a fun loving, intelligent guy
who is willing to help friends in need anytime" That's your Brand
features!

We have a name, a face, a style, a way of communicating and by
that we create different impressions and what they say about us
when we're not in the room is our Image.

So, when you want to grow in an organization, it's like a film star
who is image conscious trying to bag a good role in a movie
produced by Famous Film House.

How to Build "you" as a Brand

Whether you're on the job hunt or employed, you must think,
feel, act, plan and work like a business leader. With the rising
importance of social media, you have the responsibility to
manage your image, both virtual and in real life.

For managerial level , employers can Google before they invite
you for an interview. So if you are writing or blogging, that will
be noticed.

Decide your area of expertise and write about it on Linkedin or in
your blog. The write up should not just give ideas on your wisdom
but your imagination power and your emphasis on possibilities.

POINTS TO PONDER:

1. Which is my industry or say field? It could be Retail, Beauty,FMCG, IT , Social media, Advertising, Marketing... once decided, know experts in field, read their books, check updates about the industry or function regularly

While choosing your field/ Market, make sure that it has huge potential in future. Like Ecommerce, Digital, AI, Luxury products, Health & Beauty etc.

2. How can you describe your work? How was that done in the past and what will be its future?

3. Who is my target audience? It is HR or senior managers from the same function, so keep in touch with them. Your boss is the first senior person from your field... don't forget that and don't hesitate to seek knowledge from him/her

4. What do I do that makes me stand out from everyone else? Look at your colleagues, peers from your function/ department as Brand, too. Find out what they stand for and then set your differentiation factor.

Blog: Create your own website with a blog. 1 post of 500 words per fortnight or month discussing topics that is your expertise will help you. Share those posts via Facebook, LinkedIn, and Twitter.

Facebook Profile: Keep this simple. Updated profile photo with family is must. FB shows your personality so avoid too much commenting on politics.

LinkedIn Profile: It is your online resume, portfolio, and references.

Quora: Fairly great place to express your intelligent observations. Answer questions here which will help in building your following. Quora is a great medium to show your expertise.

Remember that for a brand to be noticed, it should be in news frequently. They advertise. You can't.

How much MONEY you have invested in yourself?

KNOWLEDGE MATRIX

	I DON'T KNOW	I KNOW
I KNOW	**I DON'T KNOW WHAT I KNOW (1)** — subconsciously we observe and know, though never give much importance to it	**I KNOW WHAT I KNOW (2)** — what we deal with regularly, we learn/ do in daily life
I DON'T KNOW	**I DON'T KNOW WHAT I DON'T KNOW (3)** — here you need someone to tell you what you must learn to achieve your dream	**I KNOW WHAT I DON'T KNOW (4)** — You are aware of this but not taking action, find out what is relevant to your career & take action

Where to invest? You need to update your knowledge regularly. The priority for you in above Matrix is No.3 & 4

You will need your seniors, colleagues to tell you on No.3 but you know for sure what you don't know!

Buying good books, attending training program or online courses, working on your personality, public speaking , mannerism or communication training programs

Take note book, add your income on left and spending on right. Know how much you have invested in yourself. If you find that you have not been investing in yourself....start doing it

Well you see most of your App's are updating their softwares regularly, some of the brands like Apple upgrade softwares and that's why they are leaders. Why not you do the same?

Earlier Mobile phones were only for voice calls, then came SMS, Camera, torch, Internet, video, movies, emails, tracking devices and now ecommerce... so now Mobile phone is market place!

How can you remain a person who knows your departments' work only? Now a sales person must know P & L, cost efficiency, Human resource management, talent development, logistics, distribution, Consumer behaviour, Marketing....

Be Jack of all and Master of one......

Within organization, how can you make yourself most visible...

• Give market / technology update feedback to seniors on regular basis, try to find some market intelligence report which is not available on google for more appreciation

• Take initiative with new projects or suggest new way of doing something that will help the company in cost efficiency

• Give feedback on new launches or new initiatives taken by your boss or seniors and try to make their initiatives successful.

• Attend relevant courses to your expertise and get Certification. Maybe join online courses from coursera or Udemy ... Inform your bosses and HR once you pass and get a certificate.

. . .

Umesh Madhyan
Associate Vice President, Logistics
at COCA-COLA
President - Chamber of Visionary
Supply Chain Leaders (CVSCL)

My motto has been always to break the shell and think beyond the role.

I would have led about 15 roles in supply chain so far in 2 decades. One of the key levers of achieving success is avoiding thinking in silos of roles, functions. It is imperative to think at a problem as an organizational problem. We often get constrained within the functional boundaries and forget to address the larger issue.

This thinking not only brings in a business centric approach, it also polishes your skills as an entrepreneur.

Below are few of the tips one can use for a successful career in Logistics:

• Technology Orientation: With the revolution of Industry 4.0 and newer technologies evolving, it becomes a basic skill to be abreast of evolving technologies. Technology awareness is something which has to work in the background while execution and diagnosing a problem. One has to be aware of pitfalls of every technology Vs. what gains it could bring in. Sometimes, it sounds like a solution could cost a bomb but a holistic end-to-end approach could result into an epiphany of paybacks.

• Creative Thinking: Technology has an answer to almost every problem – what matters is to apply it creatively and implement it appropriately. As per the Forbes survey last year, the only skill that saw a big jump from bottom 3 to top 3 skills was this. If one can't believe that there is a solution to every problem – the problem can never be solved.

• Data is the king: I've always believed Logistics = Logic + Statistics. It's all about how you use data to make a decision. Logistics is run through predicting issues in advance – not the jazzy Predictive Analytics here. It's about functional expertise and market intelligence one gets. The other aspect of data is the idea of collecting every instance of the value chain through IoT sensors. This data is so big that one will have to use Big Data on Cloud to analyse and make decision making. For instance, demand and supply variability is a key input to Replenishment. Instead of taking this as a subjective input – one can log data of every element of the chain and make it more decisive.

• Business Mindset: Logistics is the closest function within Supply Chain to the customer. What this brings in is trade-off decisions day to day on execution. One has to choose between cost inclined Vs. service inclined. These decisions can only be made once you have a strategic mindset and thought clarity of what are we trying to achieve. I strongly believe that Logistics is a function which cannot run efficiently without a signed off strategy in place. Needless to say, this strategy has to be in line with the organizational strategy.

I'm sure these tips may help one make a successful career in this ever evolving field of Logistics.

Networking is more about farming

than it is about hunting

—Ivan Misner

CHAPTER 9

NETWORKING - HELP OTHERS TO HELP YOU!

What is networking?

Networking is not just meeting with people, partying and making more friends. You don't network to bag favours from someone. It is making long term and mutually beneficial relationships with people.

Develop relationships with those in your department and in other divisions, search for potential mentors, upcoming professional opportunities, or new job opportunities that are not yet announced.

Your Network is your Net Worth

-Poter Gale

The burden is on you to take charge of your career development. Hence the importance of networking for career development too.

I was in SAP as a Key advisor-SD module. We were a big team in SAP and it gave me the opportunity to meet experts from finance, logistics, distribution, IT etc. Being from sales I had no idea on what others do.

Usually sales people feel that they run the company. Somewhat that was the case with me also!

I met Vinay Breed from Finance. It was amazing to hear him speak about his domain knowledge. He had foolproof solutions and his communication was precise and clear.

Umesh Madhyan was earlier with me as Sales Admin & Planning executive. We had a wonderful understanding. While making any analytical data, he could understand the purpose and improve the analytical criterias on his own!

He was managing sales planning / logistics but he had an excellent network within L'Oreal. Hence he would be a great help to many.

How would one help others to improve their performance... Umesh knew it very well.

Today he is Associate Vice President Logistics in Coca-Cola India

NETWORKING allows you to help others

Well you may think how helping others helps you.

That's the indirect benefit. You never know who will help you in future.

NETWORKING Gets you fresh ideas

Your network can be an excellent source of new ideas to help you. Exchanging knowledge on challenges, probable solutions is a key benefit as it allows you to gain new insights that you may not have thought of, otherwise. Similarly, you gain knowledge while finding solutions for others problems.

Moreover , it can build your reputation as an innovative thinker

NETWORKING makes you noticeable

When you stand out ' as an expert in_______'in your network , you become more visible. Nurture your networking strength and be more active in the network. Thus, construct your own career path.

The time to Build a Network is always before you need one

-Douglas Conant

Self-confidence

Interactions from networking builds self-confidence.

Start meeting new people and learn to discuss subjects they like...

How to break the ice and start a dialogue with others?

When you show interest in a subject of their liking, you will find people talk freely with you. If you are going to talk all about you, your achievements etc... no one will like to talk to you. Be assured, others have the ability to know your talent and potential.

Knowing people, preferably senior, from different divisions or departments helps. Seniors can offer you career advice, what to do and what not to do...be open to seek help from them to achieve your dream. Don't be shy of your dream.

When I returned from NIGERIA, I started working on a project called "L'Oreal Beauty Academy". I loved this idea as it was to build talent for industry as well as helping needy girls with education and job offers.

Our HR director Mohit JAMES was equally enthusiastic about the project and it was real excitement working with him. However, there was not much help from 'business' to scale up the project.

Meanwhile I met Sujata TYAGI, our HR Director ASEAN based at Singapore. She was in India earlier and hence we knew each other. I got an offer to be commercial director at MYANMAR and I accepted it quickly.

Every month when I was in India, I used to meet Mohit JAMES. In fact, India was a great time for networking.

After 2.5 years, when MYANMAR was settled in distribution, I requested Mohit to check if I can be in the Luxury Fragrances division. I felt that someone from operations is required there and Mohit agreed. Mohit worked with Sandeep KRIPLANI, the Luxury director and convinced him about me. Thus I got to be back as G.M- Luxury Div for fragrances

We have a wonderful HR team at L'OREAL and the leadership has been best in non-intrusive observation of every division team. I did have had some differences with some HR-team members but we never took it personal

That's what needs to be done.

NETWORKING doesn't mean you are meeting everyone and seeking support for your candidature. It's not political. It's basically helping each other and if you are not helping anyone, you are going nowhere.

. . .

You can be selfish but help others too!

You will have differences of opinion but you must learn to respect others' opinions, too. Learn the art of negotiations.

NETWORKING can open doors to opportunities

Ruchi Upadhyay

**Deputy General Manager Sales Marketing
at VVF Group- Softsens Consumer
Products Pvt. Limited**

Journey from Beauty Advisor(BA) to Deputy General Manager (DGM)

I still remember the day I finished my 12th exams and was asked to join as beauty advisor with Loreal. It was a very new concept as we do not use to get any formal training etc.

I gave my best and was among the top performers in west. After working for 2.5 yrs, I was promoted as supervisor, that was turning point. It prepared me for where I am right now. It gave me firsthand experience to connect with ground reality and helped me to be firm and make my roots deeper.

Working behind counters with promoters requires lot of energy, understanding and patience . You should earn the trust of team and customer ,once that is earned the sky's the limit.

Work Hard and stay humble .nothing comes easy and nothing is handed over to you .Sometimes being in right place at the right time can help ,but if you can't deliver,then it doesn't matter where you are.

I also kept my studies on ...that helped me for promotion. completing my BCOM from university,I joined my two year

Retail Management course from Welingkar's. But I was not able to give time to all, and travelling was taking a toll on my studies,So took a break, completed my course. I got selected in campus for Ozone Ayurvedics as Marketing Manager ,in 2004.

You need prioritize what is important. You cannot have all at a time, u should take risk with confidence . Do your best in whatever you do , world is full of opportunities .

I am from a Marwadi family, little orthodox, but nothing took my passion away, I still keep a veil on my head when I am with my In laws. From a girl who was not allowed to go for overnight picnic in school to now travelling the world.

You should always know to keep a balance between work and home that leads to mental satisfaction and very important for growth. Love your job ,love what you do and do it so religiously(Dil se) that no one can do it like you.

Sales was purely male dominated area ,As a women you need to work little harder as there are lot of people who makes things difficult to see your capabilty, but believe me, it just helped me to be better among the rest .Your work speaks volume and leads you to many opportunities.

I kept growing and building relationship that is key to success in any field, from start of the career. We should never forget where we came from ...that will help to to connect better and perform better.

Today I am working as DGM with VVF (Softsens Consumer Products ltd) **Job is a need for all ...but you make it a passion !**

Be positive with right approach!!!

You don't know you're going to get a 'No' until you ask, and if you don't ask, you've given yourself the No.

Jack Canfield

You don't know you're going to get a 'no' until you ask, and if you don't ask, you've given yourself the no.

—Jack Canfield

IF YOU DON'T ASK, YOU WON'T GET

"I have been working in this company sincerely and my boss knows how I work. I have got an appreciation certificate several times......Best Executive, Star Performer"The enthusiastic friend of mine was over-pouring with emotions while talking about his career achievements but still being ignored for promotions.

"Did you ask your seniors for promotion?" I asked

"They know it well," He said

"Have you confirmed if they have you in mind?"

" ? ..... ! ....."

Whether you want a good raise, you want to attend a training program or career growth, how will you get it?

If you are expecting others to keep track of your performance and give you what you want ...you're sadly mistaken.

We apply for management education, jobs and loans. When we like someone, we apply (request) for friendship (on FB) also!"Asking for work" is common in business. That's the art! So when a salesperson who's 'asking for business' from his customer all the time fails to ask ' career growth opportunity' for himself, what do you say for this ?

There are many like him that I have met, who've agreed that they feel shy of asking! We start imagining the 'result'...refusal, embarrassment, probing questions exposing our weakness, etc.

If you have the power to digest embarrassment, you can go ahead in life. Every humiliation teaches you something and makes you more mature.

> *"If you don't go after what you want, you'll never have it.*
> *If you don't ask, the answer is always no.*
> *If you don't step forward, you're always in the same place."*

—Nora Roberts

How do you get, what you want :

First and foremost, note down where you want to go next? You will learn more on this in my next tip on planning.

If you want a raise in salary, why?

Are you paid lower? Compared to peers or industry norms?

What is the difference?

List down questions and ask yourself all counter questions! Answer them all.

Company Culture

Your growth depends also on company culture. What kind of company is it? Mapping gives you answers.

One of my ASM Kartik Kamath had a fantastic track record of achievements. What I noticed was he made good use of his network. He planned 'milestone' projects & got help in special promotions from trade marketing! He was asking for help and getting it.

When you are honest & enthusiastic about your goals, people like you and support flows! You should become a source of inspiration for your colleagues.

Don't hesitate to ask, if you believe that it's going to help you perform better and you deserve it. You may not get things easily so keep on trying.

Even if you didn't get things you asked for, you will not feel frustrated later in life that "I should have asked it at that time......."

Kartik is today Regional Sales Manager and I'm sure he will be National Head one day.

Aspiring for a promotion is really important. That's a milestone in our life we want to cross. Especially first promotion is something you can't forget. There are good, bad , effective ways of asking for a promotion.

The Three things you <u>can do</u> after building aspiration for Promotion:

1. Nothing

believe in your boss or HR.

Many employees trust that their managers recognize their work and they will be faiir. Well ... when your organisation is new and growing very fast, there will be expansion of team and promotions may happen fast. You may get a promotion then, doing nothing.

There will be no competition, no fights, disputes and no disappointments for employees as everyone get the chance

Sounds like a DREAM?

2. ASK for a promotion.

That's not a good idea, too. Your boss won't like the idea that his team members asked for promotion and he had to offer it. Boss needs to get credit for it. They want 'thank you boss' from you.

Suppose you ask and your boss says 'Not at all' what next? You are out of list for an year? Maybe more

3. Resign and Hope ...

many times this idea works. If you are the best performer and your boss is dependent on your talent and team-spirit, he won't let you go.

You must check if this has happened in the company earlier. Whether your boss is good with you and you have made him dependent on yourself enough! This is a high risk effort. You must have a good offer in hand. If the boss accepts your resignation, it should not be a real shock to you.

When your CV is out in the open, mostly your HR knows it. They keep an eye on top performers and when they see you are looking out...they inform your boss.

Take help of your Boss.

That's the best way. Work with your boss.

You must have a good relationship with your boss to make this happen. (probably a prerequisite for all promotions.)

Appraisals, whether annual or mid-year is a formal review process.

Why wait for it? You have to create those opportunities to interact with your seniors more often. If you have stress, your manager has 3 X stresses, so try to find the right time and ask him / her questions...

"How am I doing? Any area that you think I should improve on?"

Be candid to tell boss your ambition to get promotion in next one year and seek honest feedback

She /He will be happy to advise.

Your seniors must know your goals, they may be happy to help you. If not, they will be compelled to say why you can't get that promotion

If you have been advised to improve on any skills, do not hesitate to ask for training on the subject, if required

Make a plan for learning to reach that goal and share with your boss Regularly ask for feedback along the way, so you can course-correct if necessary.

Do NOT surprise your boss

Don't raise questions suddenly and put your boss in a difficult situation. That's not your victory, that could be the beginning of loss of trust between you two.

Asking your boss to help you build your career will take some time.Boss will be happy to offer you a promotion. He / she will tell you how he/she fought for your promotion. Give the boss credit for it, be happy you got it.

That's always a better way to go.

Sometimes you may be Unlucky?

Let's assume that you are one of the best performers in your team. Because, without that you won't get a recommendation.

If you are working for a privately controlled company, the chances are high that professionalism is decided by the owner. For the owner, the best person is the one who is NOT paid very high and still gives great performance, doesn't raise dissenting questions on strategy etc. Here you also compete on 'Yes Sir / madam' way of working. You have to show how you care for costs and how you save/ protect owners money... whether actually that happens or not is not important.

If you are working in fair, though not fully professional organisation and you lost opportunity for promotion once. Here you must take a step back and analyze. Who got promoted and why. Have one on one meeting with boss and try to get "areas of improvement"(AOI)

Review your progress on AOI and, more importantly, get feedback on how you are progressing.

Your promotion should be sure if 'you are seen' as a person willing to learn & walk that extra mile to get that promotion.

If you did all good but still lost

May happen, whatever the results. Don't lose confidence in yourself. Sometimes there could be politics playing a greater role.

We still have this linguistic or Regional preferences in India. Also, sometimes a boss tries to bring in team members of his ex-company. Study your boss, if anything above is observed... update your CV

I advised many of my team members to go out and attend interviews for higher positions. That gives one idea of their true value and they also learn what qualities recruiters are looking for the coveted position. In case you get an offer, then what? Fine, you will be at option no.3 as stated above. Choice will be yours!

Isn't that better than not having anything in hand?

Jagdish Kini-MBA, GMP, PCC

Business Coach & Past President at ICF Bangalore Chapter
Past..
Executive Director & CEO, BHARATI AIRTEL LTD
Managing Director, GILLETTE (Wilkinson India)
Sales Director - L'Oreal India

Carving your career.

Let me start by emphasizing that you need to create and carve your careers rather than manage or predict it. "Leaders don't predict the future, they create it".

The seed for creation is a simple thought. Creation is a positive process for me, the thoughts I am referring to are only positive thoughts. Negative thoughts can only destroy and I do not believe that they could create anything. It only ensures destruction of the good done so far. To create something, one may need to dismantle or break something from the past. This means every one of us to move ahead, may need to disrupt ourselves and renew our energies to create a new path or an insight. Disruption is about getting out of the comfort zones that all of us love to be in.

While Imagination was the first part of the process, I knew I had to make these dreams come alive and give it life. I believe that when you dream in colour you actually give it life.

Giving life to your dreams is giving it energy through emotions and positive thoughts and actions. One needs the positive energy from others as well to achieve your dream. When the alignment with team and team members is complete the big goals often seem within reach.

On TRUST

You need to trust yourself and others for their abilities. Trust is not voice led; it is action led. The actions and decisions need to spell trust. Even a small doubt will show up in the actions and statements. Things are in Harmony when you trust and are in the process of trusting others. For me the best way to demonstrate trust was to show belief in the other person's strengths, capabilities and abilities.

It was easier for me to trust persons' ability and give him the onus to perform and wait for him to tell me that I was wrong. Thus, all of us have the abilities only that some of us have honed their skills faster and may be better than others. It's our application of knowledge and insights (learning's) that make us different. Most of us need to be prodded and motivated to do things, the ones who are self-motivated are the one who you see ahead, and take up leadership positions. Motivation for me came from my goals.

Be sport ....learning from it

Early in life while playing badminton or any other sports it came somewhat naturally to place the shuttle in place that would be difficult for the opponent to reach. I would imagine the shot when I was not playing and try the shot when I was actually at it. I realised the pattern that was forming in my mind.

I was imagining the shot or the end result and would push myself to achieve the result. I then understood that I need to practice the shot to consistently achieve the same result. At cricket we were made to bowl at the same spot constantly before we could stop. If the consistency was missing the coach would push us till our arms fell off. He was giving us the message, the importance of being consistent. The importance of doing it at will. Doing things at will was a form of creation; it was making things happen the way you wish.

Planning is bringing the future into the present so that you can do something about it now

–Alan Lakein

CHAPTER 11

MAKE A PERSONAL DEVELOPMENT PLAN W.R.T. INDUSTRY

Make a PLAN

You have to work on your career plan. This will be a short-term plan and Long-term plans.

Long term plan –

Industry

If you are part of a big industry, the competition is high but opportunities also are good.

Say for comparison, opportunities in the 500 crore Luxury Perfume market will be limited compared to skincare market worth 12000 crores?

Because of large market size, there will be new entrants in it and expansion by current players will be fast. That's more opportunities for employment and growth.

Select the industry accordingly..... (A)

Company

You may be happy with your current job or may not be. The happiness depends on your boss. Most people don't leave companies, they leave bosses.

Loyalty – Be loyal to your work, not company. You should work with honesty & integrity but be loyal to your career first. Your priority should be simple... you & your family

That's why we are looking for planning with respect to (w.r.t) industry and not company.

Every company has a different culture, if you spend more than 5 years in any company... you will find it difficult to leave it. You get used to its culture and then you are afraid if you will be able to manage new culture... not company.

Corporate Culture will be a critical and decisive factor in employee retention and growth.

Check your company's performance. If you have market share data or market report on ranking, you will know if your company is in growth stage, saturation level or protecting itself from losing market share.

You can make long term plans in stage- 1 & 2, but if market share is declining & everyone is seen fire-fighting, make short-term plans for the current company and identify top ranking companies to go.

You may identify the companies where you would love to work. If done so, you can put them on your network radar.

Check the app "Glassdoor" where you will get feedback on many companies, salary structures... It will help you decide your next course of action. Do not make decisions solely on any App's information. Do your homework, too.

Go with Boss

This too happens. Boss , while leaving an organisation, takes few of his trusted people with him to the new company. Be Selfish even here because your boss too is selfish getting you there! It's your career, need not be coupled with your boss all the time, unless you too have got a fantastic position and future.

Short term plan

Short term plan is the breakdown of long term plan into several steps and levels. Be clear about the next level you are planning to reach.

Where are you and where you want to go?

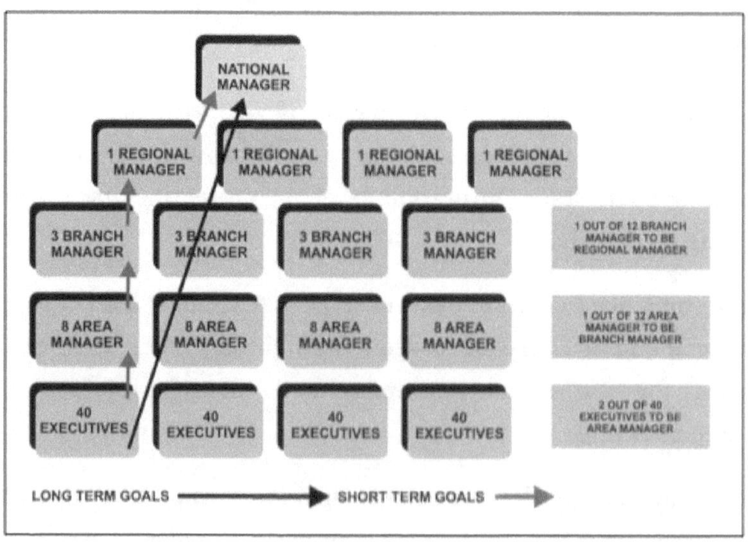

make a chart like this to give you clarity on your Goals

. . .

Know what is expected from the positions

You must check Job postings in recruitment websites or attend some interviews, so that you have JD's (Job descriptions) and KRA's (Key Responsibility Areas) for the level you want to go next

Long Term and short term, once your objectives are clear you will know what qualifications are listed by companies. It should help you plan to enrol in such courses and get the required diplomas or Degrees.

Once you have the information in hand, work out SMART goals. Hope you are aware of SMART Goals?

Specific, Measurable, Attainable and Time bound

Specific – This is setting a goal to yourself. You can set a clearly defined target for yourself like " I want to be in Marketing as Chief of Market research / analyst in FMCG sector" That's your direction

Measurable- That's quantified progress you can measure. Like " consistently delivered the research report for projects in first half 2019 before deadline and helped launch 2 products"

Attainable – Set reasonable targets . You cannot go from level 1 to level 10 in 3 years. Therefore, you have to work out reasonable targets

Relevant – every short term goal has to be relevant to a long term goal. Every input you plan to reach there, joining any training program or so, must be relevant to your Goals.

Time bound – set timelines for every short term goal and fix the review times so that you check your status against goals regularly and if required modify the plan

It is said that "when you fail to plan, you actually plan to fail"

Therefore, please make a plan, monitor the development regularly and rework process if required... without changing GOAL

The 5 P's of PLANNING

"Proper Planning Prevents Poor Performance" the 5 P's everyone must know.

I suggest these 5 P's that we learned from Mr. Jagdish Kini (we used to call him Tiger Kini) who was commercial director at L'Oreal. In the short time that I worked with him, I learned the importance of planning. He knew market very well and hence no one could fool him with stupid excuses.

"Proper planning" signifies that you make a plan which is ambitious but achievable. Your plan should give you confidence that you can achieve it.

Mr. Jagdish Kini has the power of intuition. He could predict exact sales that will be achieved in mid-month. His planning was perfect to the extent that his personal career plans were ready back then ...when will he become CEO and when will he start on his own. He followed his plan perfectly and achieved what he planned... so on professional and personal level, he is great planner

Today he is a very successful Business Coach who has trained over 300 top leaders in industry.

Thus, planning works if you are sincere about your goal and have intention to achieve it. Make a plan, but before that do proper ground work....

. . .

Introduction to Goal Setting and Action Plans

1. The first step in is determining what do you want.

2. The second step is "Looking at the bigger picture...select one want"

3. Third step is to work out what to do, how, when etc.

4. Step four is to look at your current strengths and how it will help you achieve your long and short-term goals.

5. You should make plan, start taking action with first step and celebrate success at every step.

Here are a few suggestions to help you get the most out of this book.

a) Schedule time to do your work.

b) Be honest and open. The more honest you are about what you want, the more likely it is you will obtain what you want.

c) Take your time. This SPG was not intended to be completed in an

Hour or two. Take as much time as you need.

d) Re-read your completed work

e) Review your ideas and thoughts as often as possible.

Writing Goals

There are 3 simple rules for writing goals that have a great possibility of being fulfilled. These rules are:

State your goals in the positive

Don't write what you won't do, but what you will do. See yourself as the person who is successful. Keep the word "<u>NO</u>" out of goals.

Add specifics

General goals are a great start, but adding details such as "when", "where" and "with whom" gives you a better chance of success.

Believe that you will achieve

Positive thinking is a powerful change tool. Knowing that you are capable of achieving your goals is necessary for long-term change.

Brainstorm – What Do I Want?

What do I want for myself?

Don't think about details right now. Brainstorm at least 20 wants for your-self. Get ready and brainstorm. Don't stop for at least 10 minutes or until you have at listed at least 10 wants.

1. ____

2. ____

3. ____

4. ____

5. ____

6. ____

7. ____

8. ____

9. ____

10. ____

Select the one you want the most and that you know you can achieve. Don't pick the most difficult, but the one that will be little easier to achieve and give you the confidence for next.

Re-write the want as a goal stated in the positive and with belief that you will achieve this goal.

Now add the details. Think of who, what, where, when, how much. Don't think of how, at this point, that will come soon enough.

Think Bigger

How this goal will help you achieve your long-term goal and much bigger organizational goal?

____

____

____

____

____

Identify your Strengths

There are 3 simple rules to identifying your strengths. These rules are:

Be honest Be specific Be thorough

Be honest

It is okay to admit that you have strengths. It is more than okay, it is great. It isn't bragging to say that you are good at something; it is being honest about who you are and what you are capable of doing.

Be specific

This is not the time to be wishy washy. Just as with goals, specifics help make strengths come alive. Add those details of when, who, where and others.

Be thorough

List all your strengths, not just those that are obvious to yourself or others. Little known strengths will often be as important, if not more important, that the obvious. Keep in mind that all attributes have negative and positive connotations. See if you can find the good in what you feel are some of your negatives.

One example

I am good.

A great strength, but no details are included.

I am a good and loyal friend to all people.

An example for seeing the positive in a negative

I am stubborn.

Stated like this, I am seeing being stubborn as a weakness.

I believe in what I want and am determined to get what I want.

I have changed a negative into a positive and this attribute is now strength.

Brainstorm – Recognizing Strengths

Brainstorm at least 10 of your strengths. Get ready and brainstorm. Don't stop for at least 10 minutes or until you have at listed at least 20 strengths.

1. ________________________
2. ________________________
3. ________________________
4. ________________________
5. ________________________
6. ________________________
7. ________________________
8. ________________________
9. ________________________
10. ________________________

Think about your goal. Which of these strengths will help you achieve this goal? For example, if you want to lose weight, being committed to personal achievement is a great asset. Rewrite your strengths as partners in helping you achieve your personal goal. You will use this as you write your action plans later. Try to identify at least 5 strengths that you could use to make your goals become reality. Use the format shown in the example.

Example

I will use my strength of being committed to achievement to help me in achieving my goal of losing 20 pounds in the next six months.

Now write your strengths and how they will help you achieve your goal below.

1. ________________________
2. ________________________
3. ________________________
4. ________________________
5. ________________________

Commit to a Plan

Now make a plan and select a date to start working that plan. Give your plan a name to remind you of how important this goal is to you.

Action Steps

Already you have many identified tools to help you reach your goal. You have listed your strengths and developed a big picture of your ultimate intention.

Small ways to celebrate success

Celebrate every small success...

Tell yourself how great you are

Laugh big

LET ME SUMMARIZE

First Steps – take the initiative

Coming to the conclusion part of this book.

Life is not fair. It can never be.

We all know that many successful people have gone through the toughest times in life. Success doesn't mean being a celebrity. We all can not become high profile achievers. Achieving excellence in your field is success.

There are many motivational speakers around. When you listen to them , you feel energized for some days. Then we come back to normal life. They make money, you only remember how much you paid.

Frankly you don't need any motivator to charge you. Everyone has the capacity to motivate themselves.

You take charge.

Being SELFISH is the need. Taking care of yourself and your family first.

To be successful you need to be strong first...Mentally and physically. You have to take ownership of your career and life. You have to be smart & cool. Abundance thinking will make you creative

Born in a middle class family in Mumbai, I was an average in terms of the studies. The only career that we knew at that time was medicine and engineering.

When I reached college, I realised that I have a bigger problem of understanding English. Because my Secondary Schooling was from a vernacular medium, English was difficult to follow.

I understood one thing that if at all I want to continue education , then I must improve on my English. And **I started** reading English newspapers. I started looking in the mirror and talking to myself in English. I picked up the language.

This definitely made a lot of change in me, boosting my confidence.

You need not be very fluent & master in English to succeed. But if you start working on it, you will be good at it.

The Secret of Getting Ahead is Getting Started

-Mark Twain

I was actually trapped in terms of my ambition. Like all of us.

The financial situation was bad. I had to make a decision.

So **I started** as a salesperson selling industrial switchgears. Then I moved on to join an FMCG company. At that young age, I never thought about a career. Didn't do an MBA. Just enjoyed life.

Interestingly my wife was much more positive about my career. She motivated me and hence I decided to leave Nashik and **I started** for Mumbai ...like millions who reach here for a career.

My friend B.K.Jha connected me to Laboratories GARNIER. It was an unknown brand then. Our shampoo Brand ULTRA DOUX was not selling. Failures did not deter us. We were taking returns from the market but still fighting to survive and we took the FIRST STEP to launch Hair Color (not Hair dye) in India. First time in India. No one was scared that it's a small size of market, we looked at big opportunities.

We took the first step...

The Hardest step is the first one

-Kamira Gayle

We got success in hair colours... in L'Oreal & GARNIER. This company became L'OREAL INDIA. In 22 years at L'Oreal, I really learned what the company can do in terms of people & Brand development.

For career , first level promotion is the hardest and it requires a lot of effort. You need hard work + smart work. Later, things are known. If you continue to work with the same spirit... you keep moving ahead.

Being Non-MBA, I had to do something to catch up with others. I decided to take action. **I started** reading books on management, marketing and leadership. I invested a lot into myself. Reading gave me enough knowledge & courage to speak up and debate on important issues facing the company. When learning ends, excitement ends.

I used to share my learning from every book with my team. When you teach, you master the subject yourself.

I developed my image carefully.

Despite being a Non-MBA , I could reach the position of commercial director / General Manager in L'OREAL.

I wanted to share this with young millennials and those who are hungry to grow in an organization. I meet many fresh graduates who want to be top boss within 10-15 years. Many have no idea how careers are developed along with maturity of an individual. Career is not one-day cricket or a football match.

But yes, like a sport, you have to take a first step confidently to win here. Be the first to accept change.

Take those FIRST STEPS with courage to invest in yourself.

Plan your life and career

When you plan well , you can definitely do much better.

Every decision you take will add something to your exposure, experience and knowledge.

Take that FIRST STEP towards your dream. Don't hesitate. Be bold to dream. Do not let self-doubt kill your passion.

Don't delay taking FIRST STEP towards your goal.

Any time in future, when you look back, you shouldn't regret not taking action on your dream.

www.ingramcontent.com/pod-product-compliance
Lightning Source LLC
Chambersburg PA
CBHW031342160726
47993CB00002B/795